Milo, 7 months, tester

Chiara, 20 months,
official taster

LES PETITS PLATS
FRANÇAIS
SIMON & SCHUSTER
ILLUSTRATED

baby gourmet

JENNY CARENCO

Photography by Frédéric Lucano
Styling by Sonia Lucano
Home economist Alisa Morov

SIMON &
SCHUSTER
ILLUSTRATED

London · New York · Sydney · Toronto
A CBS COMPANY

English language edition published in Great Britain by
Simon and Schuster UK Ltd, 2011
A CBS Company

Copyright © Marabout 2009

SIMON AND SCHUSTER ILLUSTRATED BOOKS
Simon & Schuster UK
222 Gray's Inn Road
London WC1X 8HB
www.simonandschuster.co.uk

1 2 3 4 5 6 7 8 9 10

Translation: Prudence Ivey
Copy editor English language: Nicki Lampon

Colour reproduction by Dot Gradations Ltd, UK
Printed and bound in U.A.E.

ISBN 978-0-85720-593-3

Every effort has been made to ensure that the information contained in this
book is complete and accurate. However, neither the publisher nor the author
are engaged in rendering professional advice or services to the individual
reader. The ideas and suggestions contained in the book are not intended
as a substitute for consultation with your healthcare provider. Neither the
publisher nor the author accept any legal responsibility for the personal
injury or other damage or loss arising from the use or misuse of the
information and advice in this book.

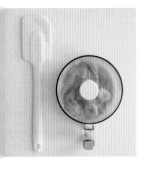

Contents

Beware of SuperMums!

It's not always easy to be a working mother. Short nights, packed public transport, empty fridge, demanding boss, partner in need of more attention… and hungry children! Therefore this book is not for the SuperMum who can do everything (Cordon Bleu cook, sex bomb, employee of the month) without ever breaking a nail. My story could be yours.

When I finished maternity leave, my daughter was only just beginning to try vegetable purées. Conditioned by 30 years of advertising, I thought of pre-packaged pots of baby food. Then I discovered that a pot containing 'green beans' was only 40% green beans; the rest was made up of potato, powdered milk, oils, salt and synthetic vitamins. Without even talking about taste, these were hardly appealing. I had a problem.

I started cooking. At first it was not ideal – coping with 2 hours of sleep while preparing my daughter's daily meals. And, instead of pretending that it's fun to cook each day for your family, I'll tell you the truth: teaching my little troupe about food taste has been a vocation. But I have done it because I was persuaded that children couldn't like healthy food if it didn't taste good.

Here I present you with my workbook. The goal: that you concentrate on one essential, to help your baby develop a taste for flavour. And when your friends stare wide-eyed at your little one devouring their broccoli, you'll say, apparently blasé but really ecstatic, 'I know, he isn't a fan of broccoli. If you could only see him with spinach…' All your efforts will be justified…

Essential tools

A hand blender – this will transform your tasty small meals into delicious soups for your baby, then into thick purées and finally into chunkier purées with morsels of whole food. Easy to use and to clean.

A vegetable peeler – better than a knife as it peels away less of the outer flesh that contains the vitamins.

A potato masher – the only thing to use to make a potato purée.

A fine sieve – to remove all lumps from purées, sauces and compotes and to drain pasta and vegetables.

Tupperware – useful for freezing, reheating, storing and washing, these will simplify your life.

Freezer bags – indispensable for freezing portions of food, keeping leftovers in the fridge or carrying snacks.

The secret to successful baby cuisine? Organisation!

Rule 1: always have a supply of 'saviour' foods

Why 'saviours'? Because if you always have them around they will be life savers, enabling you to cook healthy, quick and tasty recipes for your whole family! Without these culinary basics, you will have to keep shopping for one or two missing ingredients. So stock up regularly.

Rule 2: share recipes

Yes, you are going to cook these recipes for your baby. But think about it from another angle: the vegetables or ingredients that you are preparing for your budding gourmet can also serve as the basis for your own meal. That way you won't feel like you spend your entire evening in the kitchen, creating separate meals for your baby, your older children and you and your partner.

Rule 3: make more and work less

This will come in handy on those evenings when even the most organised don't have time to prepare a meal. Don't panic: just take one of your 'emergency boxes' that you lovingly prepared in advance out of the freezer. And if you're worried that you'll never have time to prepare these 'emergency boxes', all you have to do is make baby meals in greater quantities than you need and freeze the leftovers.

Rule 4: make a weekly meal plan

You will make your life so much easier if you manage to organise your week's menus in advance. You'll be able to do your weekly shop in one go and so cut down on the horrors of the jam-packed after-work or weekend supermarket. You'll also be able to plan recipes to work around your schedule – if Tuesday evenings are always cut short by the never-ending meeting your boss insists on holding at the last minute, use Monday evenings to calmly prepare a ratatouille... Plan so that you can make the best use of your time.

Rule 5: make Sunday evenings your ally

Use Sunday evenings to make a start on all your weekday meals. A little of your favourite music in the background will help, and just 1 hour of preparation will gain you some much needed time during the week when you are tired, stressed and irritated. Prepare all the sauces you will need, then freeze them, leaving only the accompaniments (pasta, couscous, etc.) to cook at the last minute. This Sunday evening cooking time, alone with my thoughts and my music is a truly pleasurable moment for me. And during the week when I can spend just 3 minutes heating up a pre-prepared dish I am simply ecstatic.

Store cupboard ingredients

Here are your store cupboard essentials, the groceries that you should always have to hand, that you will use regularly and that you should make sure never run out. Remember to restock them regularly.

(left to right from top)

Sultanas or raisins

Dried apricots and prunes

Ground cumin, ginger, all spice and cinnamon

Olive oil

Baking powder

Pasta

Polenta and couscous

Basmati and Arborio rice

Frozen in advance

These are your 'frozen friends', fresh groceries that have been frozen to make your life easier. They will keep for a long time but still retain their nutritional value and flavour as if just picked.

(left to right from top)

Aromatic herbs (basil, chives, tarragon, thyme and coriander) and chopped shallots and garlic

Summer berries and exotic fruits (mangoes, lychees, pineapple, etc.)

Fish fillets (cod, salmon and tuna) and white chicken meat

Green vegetables (peas, broccoli, green beans and spinach)

Fresh dairy products

This is your 'obligatory shopping basket', the things you should buy each time you go to the supermarket. They will become your instinctive purchases.

(left to right from top)

Soft cheese

Grated Parmesan cheese

Milk

Natural yoghurt

Crème fraîche

Fromage frais

Butter

Fresh fruit and veg

This is your healthy-but-tasty selection. Keep these treasures in small quantities for meals that are rich in taste and goodness. Replenish this mini-stock each week and use any other fruit and veg when in season, particularly summer berries.

(left to right from top)

Oranges and apples

Bananas

Tomatoes

Potatoes

Courgettes

Carrots

Chicken and tarragon fricassee

For 6 months onwards
Preparation time: 15 minutes
Cooking time: 15 minutes
Makes 5 x 100 g (3½ oz) portions

1 teaspoon sunflower oil
100 g (3½ oz) skinless chicken
  breast, cut into small pieces
120 g (4¼ oz) courgettes, sliced
100 g (3½ oz) turnips, peeled and
  cubed
100 g (3½ oz) broccoli florets
80 g (2¾ oz) French beans
2 teaspoons chopped fresh tarragon

Heat the oil in heavy-based saucepan and brown the pieces of chicken. Add the vegetables and tarragon then add water until the ingredients are half covered. Cook over a medium heat for 10 minutes.

Remove from the heat, drain (keeping a few spoonfuls of the cooking liquid to adjust the texture of the purée if necessary) then blend until you have a smooth purée.

Add a little of the cooking liquid if the mixture is too dense or grainy.

Variation: Chicken stuffed with tarragon and Parma ham: You will need a 150 g (5¼ oz) chicken breast per person. Cut a pocket in each chicken breast at its thickest point, opening it without cutting it completely in two. Cook the vegetables with the tarragon as in the recipe above, drain and blend to form a dense purée. Place each chicken breast on a slice of Parma ham, spoon a portion of the vegetable purée into the pocket, close the pocket and wrap the ham around the chicken, securing it with a couple of toothpicks. Cook at 200°C (fan oven 180°C), Gas Mark 6, for 10–12 minutes. Remove the toothpicks before serving and cut the chicken in two to reveal the pretty stuffing. Serve with a mixed green salad and some bread spread with goat's cheese.

Little lamb stew with green vegetables

For 6 months onwards
Preparation time: 10 minutes
Cooking time: 25 minutes
Makes 5 x 100 g (3½ oz) portions

1 teaspoon sunflower oil
100 g (3½ oz) lamb shoulder or leg,
   cut into small pieces
100 g (3½ oz) turnips, peeled and
   cut into small pieces
30 g (1 oz) celeriac, peeled and cut
   into small pieces
60 g (2 oz) courgette, cut into small
   pieces
75 g (2½ oz) peas
75 g (2½ oz) French beans
50 g (1¾ oz) broccoli florets

Heat the oil in a lidded heavy-based saucepan and brown the lamb. Add the turnips and celeriac, half cover with water, put the lid on and leave to simmer for 15 minutes. Add the green vegetables and cook for a further 10 minutes.

Remove from the heat and blend until you have a smooth purée.

Serve with Cauliflower purée (see page 22).

Variation: For a family of four, use 100 g (3½ oz) of lamb per person and double the remaining quantities in the recipe. When you add the turnip and celeriac, also add a chicken stock cube, 1 crushed garlic clove and a teaspoon of chopped fresh thyme. Before serving, season with sea salt and freshly ground black pepper to taste.

Sole with courgettes and broad beans

For 6 months onwards
Preparation time: 10 minutes
Cooking time: 15 minutes
Makes 5 x 100 g (3½ oz) portions

3–4 sole fillets (around 100g/3½ oz
  each)
1 teaspoon olive oil
½ garlic clove, crushed
2 teaspoons shallots, finely
  chopped
200 g (7 oz) courgettes, sliced
150 g (5¼ oz) broad beans, shelled
  and skinned (fresh or frozen)

Make sure there are no bones in the fish.

Heat the oil in a lidded saucepan and brown the garlic and shallots. Add the courgettes and broad beans and cook for around 8 minutes.

Place the sole fillets on top of the vegetables, cover and cook for around 2–3 minutes.

Remove from the heat and check that 2–3 dessertspoons of cooking liquid are left at the bottom of the saucepan. If not, pour some out or add a little water to get the right quantity.

Blend until you have a smooth purée.

Serve with Sweet potato purée (see page 24) or Pumpkin purée (see page 23).

Tip: If you can't find broad beans you can replace them with garden peas.

Variation: This recipe can easily be adapted to feed the whole family – use the ingredients to make a delicious fish pie with sweet potato topping. Place the courgettes, broad beans, garlic, shallots, a few drops of lemon juice and some basil in a casserole dish. Place the raw sole fillets (allow 2–3 per person according to their size) on top of the vegetables and cover with a layer of mashed sweet potatoes (see page 24). Cook at 200°C (fan oven 180°C), Gas Mark 6 for 20 minutes.

Italian beef ragù

For 6 months onwards
Preparation time: 5 minutes
Cooking time: 25 minutes
Makes 5 x 100 g (3½ oz) portions

1 teaspoon olive oil
½ garlic clove, chopped
100 g (3½ oz) stewing beef (neck or shoulder), cut into small pieces
70 g (2½ oz) carrots, peeled, cut into small pieces
20 g (¾ oz) tomatoes, skinned, cut into small pieces
120 g (4¼ oz) courgettes, cut into small pieces
20 g (¾ oz) celery, cut into small pieces
2 teaspoons tomato purée
½ teaspoon chopped fresh thyme

Heat the oil in a lidded heavy-based saucepan and brown the garlic and beef. Add the vegetables, tomato purée, thyme and 100 ml (3½ fl oz) of water. Cover and leave to simmer for 25 minutes.

Remove from the heat and blend until the ragù has a smooth texture.

Serve with Parsnip purée (see page 25) or Avocado purée (see page 29).

Salmon with spinach

For 6 months onwards
Preparation time: 5 minutes
Cooking time: 15 minutes
Makes 5 x 100 g (3½ oz) portions

100 g (3½ oz) salmon fillet, cubed
1 teaspoon lemon juice
500 g (1 lb 2 oz) frozen spinach
  (preferably organic)
2 dessertspoons crème fraîche

Put the salmon on a plate and check that there are no bones. Sprinkle the salmon with the lemon juice. Set aside.

Put the spinach in a saucepan and pour over water until it is just covered. Bring to the boil then leave to cook for 10 minutes. Add the salmon cubes and cook for a further 5 minutes.

Drain and return the saucepan to the heat. Add the crème fraîche, mix well and allow to heat through.

Blend to a smooth purée.

Serve with Potato purée (see page 31) or Turnip purée (see page 30).

Variation: This dish will work just as well with white fish such as cod or sole. If using these, omit the lemon juice as it can overpower the delicate flavour of white fish.

Cauliflower purée

For 6 months onwards
Preparation time: 7 minutes
Cooking time: 15 minutes
Makes 5 x 100 g (3½ oz) portions

200 ml (7 fl oz) milk
600 g (1 lb 5 oz) cauliflower florets
   (fresh or frozen)
10 g (¼ oz) butter

Bring the milk to the boil, add the cauliflower and cook over a medium heat for 15 minutes (be careful as the milk will boil over the pan very easily).

Drain off the milk, reserving it.

Blend the cauliflower with the butter, adding a little of the cooking milk to get a smooth purée.

Variation: Add a sprig of thyme 5 minutes before the end of the cooking time and remove before blending. This will add sweetness without overpowering the taste of the cauliflower.

Pumpkin purée

or 6 months onwards (4 months if
butter removed)
Preparation time: 10 minutes
Cooking time: 15 minutes
Makes 5 x 100 g (3½ oz) portions

50 g (1 lb 10 oz) pumpkin, peeled,
de-seeded and cubed
large floury potato, peeled and
cubed
0 g (¼ oz) butter
–3 drops lemon juice

Place the vegetables in a saucepan,
cover with water, bring to the boil and
leave to cook for 15 minutes. Drain.

Blend with the butter and lemon juice
until you have a very smooth purée.

Tip: Pumpkin can sometimes taste a
little 'earthy'. Lemon juice adds the
touch of acidity needed to balance
and lift the natural flavour.

Variation: This is even better with a
little vanilla or a pinch of cumin. Add
fresh vanilla seeds or ¼ teaspoon of
ground cumin to the mixture just
before blending.

Sweet potato purée

For 6 months onwards (4 months if butter removed)
Preparation time: 5 minutes
Cooking time: 15 minutes
Makes 5 x 100 g (3½ oz) portions

600 g (1 lb 5 oz) sweet potatoes, peeled and cubed
10 g (¼ oz) butter

Put the sweet potatoes in a saucepan, cover with water, bring to the boil and cook for 15 minutes. Drain.

Mash with the butter until you have a very smooth purée.

Tip: Sweet potatoes are sweet, as their name implies, and loved by babies. For older infants I like to cut the sweet potatoes into batons and roast them for around 20 minutes. The flavour becomes even more pronounced and the kids love to eat them with their fingers.

Parsnip purée

For 6 months onwards
Preparation time: 10 minutes
Cooking time: 15 minutes
Makes 5 x 100 g (3½ oz) portions

600 g (1 lb 5 oz) parsnips, peeled
and cubed
200 ml (7 fl oz) milk
10 g (¼ oz) butter

Put the parsnips and milk in a saucepan, bring to the boil and cook for 15 minutes. Drain, keeping a little of the cooking milk aside.

Blend with the butter and a little of the milk until you have a smooth, creamy purée.

Variation: You can vary this recipe by replacing 1 parsnip with a sweet apple. Add the peeled, cored and cubed apple 5 minutes before the end of the cooking time. Drain the excess milk so that the purée is not too liquid then blend. For older children, serve it with beef bourguignon or lamb cutlets.

Broccoli purée

For 4 months onwards
Preparation time: 7 minutes
Cooking time: 10 minutes
Makes 5 x 100 g (3½ oz) portions

600 g (1 lb 5 oz) broccoli florets
   (fresh or frozen)
1 teaspoon olive oil

Put the broccoli in a saucepan, half cover with water, bring to the boil and leave to cook without covering for 10 minutes. There should only be a very little water left after cooking, around 2 tablespoonfuls.

Blend the broccoli with the remaining cooking water and the oil.

Variations: To make this strong purée sweeter and more creamy for a baby of 6 months onwards, add 2 soft cheese triangles just before blending.

You could also add a small handful of fresh flat leaf parsley or sage before blending.

Pea purée

For 6 months onwards
Preparation time: 5 minutes
Cooking time: 7–8 minutes
Makes 5 x 100 g (3½ oz) portions

500 g (1 lb 2 oz) frozen peas
2 dessertspoons crème fraîche

Put the peas in a saucepan, cover with water, bring to the boil and leave to cook for 7–8 minutes. Drain.

Blend with the crème fraîche until you have a smooth purée.

Tip: Some babies don't like grainy textures. I believe that they should get used to the natural textures of food but, if you have to, pass the purée through a fine sieve to get a smoother mixture.

Variation: For a slightly tangy note, blend with 2 fresh mint leaves. This is delicious with grilled lamb.

French bean purée

For 4 months onwards
Preparation time: 5 minutes
Cooking time: 10 minutes
Makes 5 x 100 g (3½ oz) portions

500 g (1 lb 2 oz) French beans
(fresh or frozen), topped and tailed
if necessary
1 teaspoon olive oil

Put the beans in a saucepan, half cover with water, bring to the boil and leave to cook without covering for 10 minutes. There should only be a very little water left after cooking, around 2 tablespoonfuls.

Blend the beans with the cooking water and olive oil.

Variations: Replace half the beans with peas and pass the purée through a fine sieve. This makes it a little sweeter and runnier than the 100% bean version.

For a summery flavour, add 2 fresh basil leaves before blending. It will work perfectly with both versions of this green purée.

Avocado purée

For 4 months onwards
Preparation time: 5 minutes
Makes 1 x 100 g (3½ oz) portion

1 ripe avocado, stoned
2–3 drops lemon juice

Scoop out the avocado flesh and put in a bowl.

Add the lemon juice to preserve the green colour then blend.

Tips: Unlike other fruits, avocados ripen once picked, not on the tree. A hard avocado is therefore a fresh avocado. To ripen, simply leave at room temperature in a brown paper bag. To speed up the process, place it next to a banana or an apple.

My daughter Maya still devours this purée with chicken, grilled meat or fish such as tuna or swordfish. Now she's older, we add a tiny pinch of sea salt and a drop of Tabasco to make a kid's guacamole.

Turnip purée

For 6 months onwards
Preparation time: 10 minutes
Cooking time: 15 minutes
Makes 5 x 100 g (3½ oz) portions

500 g (1 lb 2 oz) turnips, peeled and cubed
10 g (¼ oz) butter

Put the turnips in a lidded saucepan, half cover with water, cover and leave to cook for 15 minutes.

Drain and blend with the butter.

Potato purée

For 6 months onwards
Preparation time: 10 minutes
Cooking time: 15 minutes
Makes 5 x 100 g (3½ oz) portions

400 g (14 oz) potatoes, peeled and
  cubed
100 ml (3½ fl oz) milk
10 g (¼ oz) butter

Put the potatoes in a saucepan, cover with water and leave to cook for 15 minutes.

Drain and mash with the milk and butter.

Tip: Never blend potatoes in a blender or food processor. They will become glue-like and inedible because of their high starch content.

Fine orange semolina

For 9 months onwards
Preparation time: 5 minutes
Cooking time: 5 minutes
Makes 1 x 100 g (3½ oz) portion

70 ml (2½ fl oz) orange juice
50 g (1¾ oz) fine semolina

Bring the orange juice to the boil in a lidded saucepan.

Away from the heat add the semolina, stir, cover and leave to soak for 5 minutes.

Remove the lid and run a fork through the semolina before serving.

Serve with Vegetable tagine (see page 34) or Ratatouille (see page 35).

Tip: If the semolina is too dry for your baby and causes them trouble swallowing, add 100 ml (3½ fl oz) of orange juice and 2 tablespoons of carrot purée to moisten it. If you serve it like this, you can make several servings in advance and freeze them.

Vegetable tagine

For 9 months onwards
Preparation time: 10 minutes
Cooking time: 20 minutes
Makes 5 x 100 g (3½ oz) portions

2 teaspoons olive oil
½ garlic clove, chopped
a small pinch of ground ginger
a small pinch of ground cumin
a small pinch of finely chopped
    fresh coriander
4 dried apricots, chopped
120 g (4¼ oz) courgettes, chopped
100 g (3½ oz) carrots, peeled and
    chopped
200 g (7 oz) tomatoes, chopped
50 g (1¾ oz) aubergine, chopped
1 dessertspoon tomato purée

Heat the oil in a lidded heavy-based saucepan and cook the garlic until golden. Add the spices, coriander and apricots. Stir and leave to cook for 1 minute.

Add the vegetables, tomato purée and 100 ml (3½ fl oz) of water and bring to the boil. Lower the heat, cover and leave to simmer over a low heat for 15 minutes.

Remove from the heat and blend until fairly smooth.

Serve with Fine orange semolina (see page 32).

Tip: If your baby isn't used to spices, introduce them slowly. The first time you make this, replace the ginger with a few drops of lemon and add just a tiny amount of cumin. You can gradually increase the quantities of spice until your baby is used to them.

Ratatouille

or 9 months onwards
Preparation time: 10 minutes
Cooking time: 20 minutes
Makes 5 x 100 g (3½ oz) portions

teaspoons olive oil
½ garlic clove, chopped
teaspoons finely chopped shallots
80 g (6¼ oz) courgettes, chopped
00 g (7 oz) tomatoes, chopped
0 g (1¾ oz) aubergine, chopped
dessertspoon tomato purée
small pinch of dried thyme

Heat the oil in a lidded heavy-based saucepan and cook the garlic and shallots until golden. Add the vegetables, tomato purée, thyme and 100 ml (3½ fl oz) of water and bring to the boil. Reduce the heat, cover and leave to simmer for 15 minutes.

Remove from the heat and blend coarsely.

Serve with Fine orange semolina (see page 32).

Variation: For a luxurious take on this recipe, you could use skinned cherry tomatoes instead of normal ones. Use them whole so that they release their juices at the end of the cooking time and do not become overcooked.

Pasta shapes with soft cheese and basil

For 9 months onwards
Preparation time: 5 minutes
Cooking time: 8 minutes
Makes 1 x 100 g (3½ oz) portion

100 g (3½ oz) small pasta shapes
　(such as alphabet shapes or stars)
1 rounded teaspoon soft cheese
a few fresh basil leaves, finely
　chopped

Cook the pasta according to the packet instructions.

Drain and return to the pan.

Add the cheese and basil, stir and return to the heat until the cheese has melted.

Serve with Primavera sauce (see page 38), Fresh tomato sauce (see page 39), Creamy spinach (see page 40) or Broad beans, ricotta and basil (see page 41).

Tip: If possible, use wholewheat pasta. This has a high nutritional value and a delicious slightly nutty flavour. As it is high in fibre it will also aid digestion.

ROMEO

Primavera sauce

For 9 months onwards
Preparation time: 10 minutes
Cooking time: 15 minutes
Makes 5 x 100 g (3½ oz) portions

2 teaspoons olive oil
2 teaspoons finely chopped shallots
120 g (4¼ oz) courgettes, chopped
100 g (3½ oz) French beans,
  quartered
100 g (3½ oz) frozen peas
100 g (3½ oz) broccoli florets
3 dessertspoons crème fraîche

Heat the oil in a lidded, heavy-based saucepan and cook the shallots until golden.

Add the vegetables, half cover with water and bring to the boil. Lower the heat, cover and leave to cook for 10 minutes.

Drain the vegetables, reserving around 3 tablespoons of cooking liquid. Return the vegetables to the pan, add the crème fraîche and heat with some of the reserved liquid.

Blend to a coarse purée, adding more cooking liquid if necessary.

Serve with Pasta shapes with soft cheese and basil (see page 36) but use half fat crème fraîche to make it less rich.

Tip: I often use frozen vegetables to speed up preparation time. They are usually good quality.

Fresh tomato sauce

For 9 months onwards
Preparation time: 5 minutes
Cooking time: 20 minutes
Makes 5 x 100 g (3½ oz) portions

2 teaspoons olive oil
½ garlic clove, finely chopped
600 g (1 lb 5 oz) tomatoes, skinned
(preferably cherry tomatoes),
quartered

Heat the oil in a lidded heavy-based saucepan and cook the garlic until golden.

Add the tomatoes, reduce the heat, cover and leave to cook over a medium heat for 15–20 minutes depending on the size of the tomatoes.

Remove from the heat and blend, leaving some lumps for texture.

Serve with Pasta shapes with soft cheese and basil (see page 36).

Tip: This is cheating a little, but if you find tomatoes too acidic, add 1 dessertspoon of tomato ketchup to the sauce.

Creamy spinach

For 9 months onwards
Preparation time: 5 minutes
Cooking time: 10 minutes
Makes 5 x 100 g (3½ oz) portions

500 g (1 lb 2 oz) frozen spinach
  (preferably organic)
2 dessertspoons crème fraîche

Put the spinach in a lidded saucepan, half cover with water, cover the pan with a lid and bring to the boil. Reduce the heat and cook over a medium heat for 10 minutes.

Drain thoroughly (spinach retains lots of water). Add the crème fraîche and return to the saucepan to heat through.

Blend to a rough purée.

Serve with Pasta shapes with soft cheese and basil (see page 36).

Tip: This recipe, served with pasta, is a typical Scandinavian dish that may seem a surprising combination. I can assure you, however, that it is simply delicious. There is a slightly acidic note in both the spinach and the crème fraîche that goes brilliantly with different types of pasta. When I eat with the kids, I roast a salmon fillet in the oven to eat with it.

Broad beans, ricotta and basil

For 9 months onwards
Preparation time: 5 minutes
Cooking time: 15 minutes
Makes 5 x 100 g (3½ oz) portions

400 g (14 oz) broad beans, skinned
½ vegetable stock cube
1 small courgette, finely chopped
2 dessertspoons ricotta
a few fresh basil leaves, finely
  chopped

Put the broad beans in a lidded saucepan, cover with water, crumble in the stock cube, cover and bring to the boil. Reduce the heat and cook for 10 minutes. Add the courgette and cook for a further 5 minutes.

Drain, leaving about 3 dessertspoons of liquid in the pan.

Away from the heat, mix the vegetables with the ricotta and basil.

Serve with Pasta shapes with soft cheese and basil (see page 36) but omit the soft cheese from the pasta.

Variation: Use goat's cheese instead of ricotta.

Pumpkin, sweet potato and vanilla soup

For 9 months onwards
Preparation time: 10 minutes
Cooking time: 20 minutes
Makes 5 x 200 g (7 oz) portions

300 g (10½ oz) pumpkin, peeled, de-seeded and chopped
2 large sweet potatoes, peeled and chopped
1 vanilla pod
2 dessertspoons crème fraîche
2 teaspoons lemon juice

Put the vegetables in a large lidded saucepan and add 700 ml (1¼ pints) of water. Split the vanilla pod open lengthways, scrape the seeds into the pan, then add the pod.

Bring to the boil. Cover and leave to cook over a medium heat for 20 minutes.

Take off the heat and remove the vanilla pod.

Add the crème fraîche and the lemon juice then blend.

Tip: The soup should be fairly runny. If it is too thick, add a little water. If it is too liquid, boil some sweet potato or potato, add to the mixture and blend again.

Variation: This soup is an excellent way to introduce your baby to mushrooms. For Maya, I finely chopped some mushrooms and cooked them in a bit of butter. I added them to the centre of the soup and she loved them. Now she'll even eat raw mushrooms happily.

Broccoli and soft cheese soup

For 9 months onwards
Preparation time: 5 minutes
Cooking time: 10 minutes
Makes 5 x 200 g (7 oz) portions

1 teaspoon olive oil
2 teaspoons finely chopped shallots
400 g (14 oz) broccoli florets
4 rounded teaspoons soft cheese

Heat the oil in a lidded heavy-based saucepan and cook the shallots for 1 minute or until they are translucent. Add the broccoli and 700 ml (1¼ pints) of water. Reduce the heat, cover and leave to cook for 10 minutes.

Away from the heat, add the soft cheese and blend.

Serve with some fresh bread if your baby likes it.

Tip: The soup should be fairly runny. If it is too thick, add a little water. If it is too liquid, boil some broccoli florets, add them to the soup and blend again.

Variation: For infants over 1 year, add a few finely crushed walnuts. You can also leave a few whole broccoli florets in the soup to give their new teeth something to chew on.

Creamed sweetcorn and tomatoes

For 9 months onwards
Preparation time: 5 minutes
Cooking time: 20 minutes
Makes 5 x 200 g (7 oz) portions

300 g (10½ oz) frozen sweetcorn (if you can't find frozen you could use tinned corn but this is more sugary)
6 large tomatoes, skinned and quartered
4 fresh sage leaves, chopped
2 dessertspoons crème fraîche

Put the sweetcorn, tomatoes and sage in a saucepan, add 700 ml (1¼ pints) of water and bring to the boil. Cover and leave to cook for 15 minutes.

Remove from the heat, add the crème fraîche and blend.

Tips: The soup should be quite runny. If it is too thick add a little water. If it is too liquid, add some corn directly to the mixture, cook for 5–7 minutes then blend.

Older babies will enjoy having the corn left whole to give them something to crunch.

Italian meatballs

For 12 months onwards
Preparation time: 20 minutes
Cooking time: 25 minutes
Makes 5 x 120 g (4¼ oz) portions

Meatballs
100 g (3½ oz) minced beef
½ onion, finely chopped
1 potato, cooked and mashed
ground pepper to taste

Tomato sauce
2 teaspoons olive oil
1 teaspoon finely chopped garlic
6 large tomatoes, skinned and
   quartered
1 dessertspoon tomato purée
4 fresh basil leaves, chopped

Mix together the beef, onion, potato and pepper. Make small balls (the mixture should be enough for around 15) and leave to stand for 10–15 minutes at room temperature.

Heat half the olive oil in a lidded heavy-based saucepan and cook the garlic until lightly golden but not brown. Add the tomatoes, tomato purée and basil. Cover and leave to simmer for 10 minutes.

In another pan, heat the rest of the oil and carefully add the meatballs. Brown on all sides so that they are sealed and you can't see any raw meat around the outside.

Remove the tomato sauce from the heat and blend. Add the meatballs and cook over a very low heat, simmering for around 10 minutes until the meatballs are cooked through.

Serve these meatballs with little cooked pasta shapes sprinkled with some grated Parmesan cheese.

Tip: I must admit that sometimes I find it far too laborious and time consuming to make these meatballs myself. I often use frozen meatballs instead. There's nothing easier than just heating them through in the tomato sauce for 10 minutes.

Chicken and vegetables in coconut milk

For 12 months onwards
Preparation time: 15 minutes
Cooking time: 15 minutes
Makes 5 x 120 g (4¼ oz) portions

1 dessertspoon sunflower oil
100 g (3½ oz) skinless chicken
  breast, cut into small pieces
1 garlic clove, finely chopped
½ teaspoon ground ginger
2 carrots, peeled and sliced
1 courgette, sliced
100 g (3½ oz) French beans, cut
  into small pieces
5–6 broccoli florets
200 g (7 oz) creamed coconut
juice of ½ a lemon
3–4 fresh coriander leaves,
  chopped

Heat the sunflower oil in a large, lidded, heavy-based saucepan and brown the pieces of chicken.

Add the garlic and ginger and continue cooking for 1 minute.

Add the vegetables, coconut, lemon juice and 500 ml (18 fl oz) of water. Cover and leave to simmer over a low heat for 15 minutes.

Remove from the heat, add the coriander and blend very roughly.

Tip: Serve with basmati rice. For one portion, boil 100 ml (3½ fl oz) of water in a saucepan. Add 50 g (1¾ oz) of rice, cover and cook over a low heat for 15 minutes or until the water is completely absorbed.

If your baby doesn't like coconut you could replace it with crème fraîche, leaving out the lemon juice as crème fraîche has a slightly acidic flavour.

Pasta with ham and peas

For 12 months onwards
Preparation time: 2 minutes
Cooking time: 7 minutes
Makes 1 x 120 g (4¼ oz) portion

100 g (3½ oz) pasta shapes
50 g (1¾ oz) peas
a small knob of butter
1 teaspoon finely chopped shallots
1 ham slice, cut into small pieces
2 dessertspoons crème fraîche

Cook the pasta according to the packet instructions.

Meanwhile, bring a small pan of water to the boil and cook the peas for 5 minutes. Drain and return to the pan.

Return the pan to the heat and add the butter, shallots and ham. Leave to cook for 1–2 minutes, stirring constantly.

Add the crème fraîche and bring to the boil, then take off the heat.

Drain the pasta. Serve topped with the pea and ham sauce.

Tip: To make this even faster, have a supply of finely chopped shallots (and garlic and onion) in your freezer. If you do this you won't even need a chopping board for this delicious but simple pasta dish.

Tuna niçoise with thyme semolina

For 12 months onwards
Preparation time: 2 minutes
Cooking time: 5 minutes
Makes 1 x 120 g (4¼ oz) portion

100 g (3½ oz) Ratatouille (see page 35)
20 g (¾ oz) canned tuna, drained and flaked
½ teaspoon dried thyme
50 g (1¾ oz) fine semolina

Heat the ratatouille, add the tuna and mix together. Reduce the heat and leave to cook for 5 minutes.

Meanwhile, bring 500 ml (18 fl oz) of water to the boil. Add the thyme and semolina. Cover and leave to soak for 5 minutes.

Stir the semolina with a fork and serve with the tuna ratatouille.

Tip: This dish can also be made with Fresh tomato sauce (see page 39), which you have – of course – prepared in advance and can just take out of your freezer.

Corn and carrot cheesy fritters

For 12 months onwards
Preparation time: 10 minutes
Cooking time: 20 minutes
Makes 5 x 200 g (7 oz) portions or
20 fritters

Fritters
400 g (14 oz) carrots, peeled and
sliced
200 g (7 oz) sweetcorn
200 g (7 oz) Comté cheese, grated
½ teaspoon paprika
1 teaspoon olive oil

Avocado purée
½ ripe avocado
a few drops of lemon juice

Put the carrots in a saucepan and cover with water. Bring to the boil and leave to cook for 10 minutes. Add the sweetcorn and cook for a further 5–7 minutes.

Drain the vegetables. Add the cheese and paprika and mix until the cheese starts to melt. Mash to a rough paste.

Make the mixture into small flat fritters around 3 cm (1¼ inches) in diameter and 1 cm (½ inch) thick. Leave to rest for a few minutes on kitchen towel so they are not too moist.

Heat the oil in a non-stick pan and cook the fritters for 3–5 minutes on each side. Leave to cool on more kitchen towel.

At the last minute, put the avocado flesh into a bowl with the lemon juice. Mash with a fork until you have a smooth purée.

Serve the fritters (a portion will have around 4) with the avocado purée. Let your baby eat with their fingers so they can dunk the fritters in the purée.

Tip: These fritters make a perfect starter for dinner with friends. Just cook them for a little longer so that they are more crispy. Serve with guacamole (2 mashed ripe avocados mixed with 1–2 finely chopped chillies, 1 finely chopped tomato, ½ finely chopped red onion, some lime juice, chopped coriander and seasoning). Dunk without moderation.

Polenta batons with a tomato and red pepper relish

For 12 months onwards

Preparation time: 10 minutes + cooling

Cooking time: 30 minutes

Makes 5 x 100 g (3½ oz) portions of tomato and red pepper relish and 1 x 120 g (4¼ oz) portion of polenta

Tomato and red pepper relish

5 vine tomatoes or 20 cherry tomatoes, skinned, quartered and de-seeded

2 red peppers, de-seeded and thinly sliced

1 tablespoon olive oil

Polenta

100 ml (3½ fl oz) milk

50 g (1¾ oz) dried polenta

20 g (¾ oz) Parmesan cheese, grated

Preheat the oven to 150°C (fan oven 130°C), Gas Mark 2.

Spread the tomatoes and peppers on a baking tray covered with foil. Drizzle with the olive oil. Roast in the middle of the oven for 30 minutes.

Take out of the oven and leave to cool. Blend or roughly chop according to your baby's taste.

Bring the milk to the boil in a pan. Remove from the heat and add the polenta and Parmesan, mixing vigorously until you have a thick paste. Pour on to a plate or tray to form a 1 cm (½ inch) thick square. Leave to cool then cut into batons.

Serve the polenta with the tomato and red pepper relish.

Tip: I always set aside a little of the tomato and red pepper relish to use as a chutney for the grown ups. It is delicious and goes really well with cheese, white meat or grilled salmon.

Variation: In season, feel free to add a few apricots to roast with the vegetables.

Fusilli with summer vegetables and basil

For 12 months onwards
Preparation time: 5 minutes
Cooking time: 10 minutes
Makes 1 x 230 g (8 oz) portion

1 dessertspoon olive oil
1 teaspoon finely chopped garlic
3 cherry tomatoes, skinned and
  halved
½ courgette, sliced
¼ red pepper, de-seeded and
  chopped
3–4 fresh basil leaves, finely
  chopped
60 g (2 oz) fusilli

Heat the oil in a heavy-based saucepan and add the garlic. Cook for 1 minute then add the vegetables and basil. Cook for a further 10 minutes over a medium heat.

Cook the pasta according to the packet instructions. Drain then mix with the vegetable sauce.

Variation: Chop a few green olives and a few slices of strong chorizo. Mix with the vegetables for a delicious dinner for Mum and Dad.

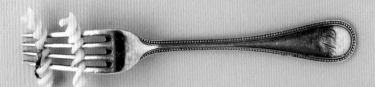

Penne with sugar snap peas and pesto

For 12 months onwards
Preparation time: 5 minutes
Cooking time: 10 minutes
Makes 1 x 230 g (8 oz) portion

1 tablespoon olive oil
1 small garlic clove
5–6 basil leaves
1 dessertspoon pine nuts
1 dessertspoon grated Parmesan
cheese
100 g (3½ oz) sugar snap peas or
mange tout, cut into small pieces
50 g (2 oz) penne

Using a food processor or blender, blend the oil, garlic, basil, pine nuts and Parmesan to a smooth pesto.

Bring a small pan of water to the boil and cook the sugar snap peas or mange tout for 7–10 minutes.

Cook the penne according to the packet instructions.

Drain the penne, then mix with the sugar snap peas and pesto. My daughter finds this dish very amusing as the penne could be made to measure to fit on her fingers.

Tip: For the grown ups, sprinkle this dish with shavings of fresh Parmesan and pine nuts that you have toasted in a non-stick pan.

61

Farfalle with broccoli and Parmesan

For 12 months onwards
Preparation time: 5 minutes
Cooking time: 10 minutes
Makes 1 x 230 g (8 oz) portion

100 g (3½ oz) broccoli florets
1 dessertspoon olive oil
1 teaspoon finely chopped shallots
60 g (2 oz) farfalle
2 dessertspoons grated Parmesan
cheese

Bring a pan of water to the boil, add the broccoli and leave to cook for 5–7 minutes. Drain and set aside.

Heat the oil in the same pan and add the shallots. Cook for 1 minute then add the broccoli. Cook for a few minutes. Remove from the heat, add the Parmesan, reheat and set aside.

Cook the farfalle according to the packet instructions.

Drain, then mix the pasta with the broccoli mixture. This is best eaten with your baby's favourite fork.

Variation: This recipe is simple and will work with almost all green vegetables. For a touch of sophistication, add 1 teaspoon of grated lemon zest, 1 dessertspoon of lemon juice and a few fresh sage leaves. This is sure to impress your mother-in-law when she drops in unexpectedly on a Sunday evening...

Pasta with cherry tomatoes and mozzarella

or 12 months onwards
Preparation time: 5 minutes
Cooking time: 10 minutes
Makes 1 x 230 g (8 oz) portion

1 dessertspoon olive oil
1 teaspoon finely chopped garlic
5 cherry tomatoes, skinned and
  halved
½ mozzarella ball, cubed
60 g (2 oz) pasta
3–4 fresh fresh basil leaves, finely
  chopped

Heat the oil in a heavy-based saucepan and add the garlic. Cook for 1 minute then add the tomatoes and cook for a further 5 minutes over a medium heat.

Remove from the heat, add the mozzarella, return to the heat and leave until the mozzarella is beginning to melt.

Cook the pasta according to the packet instructions.

Drain, then mix with the tomatoes and mozzarella and sprinkle with the basil leaves.

Variation: If your baby's dinner has made your mouth water, grill a few slices of Parma ham, cut into pieces and serve with the pasta. A delicacy.

Mango and banana compote

For 4 months onwards
Preparation time: 10 minutes
Cooking time: 10 minutes
Makes 5 x 100 g (3½ oz) portions

2 ripe mangoes or 400 g (14 oz)
    mango flesh (see Tip)
3 bananas, sliced

Cut the mangoes in half. With a small knife, remove the skin from both halves and cut the flesh into pieces. Cut off the flesh around the stone.

Put the fruit in a saucepan, half cover with water and bring to the boil. Cover and leave to cook for 10 minutes. When done, there should be about 3 dessertspoons of liquid remaining.

Blend to a smooth purée.

Tip: Frozen mango, available skinned and sliced, is less expensive and more practical to use than fresh.

Pineapple and lychee compote

For 6 months onwards
Preparation time: 15 minutes
Cooking time: 20 minutes
Makes 5 x 100 g (3½ oz) portions

2 pineapples or around 300 g
  (10½ oz) pineapple flesh (see Tip)
200 g (7 oz) lychees (fresh or
  frozen, but not canned as they are
  far too sugary)

Peel the pineapple until there is not the slightest trace of skin on the flesh. Cut around the hard stalk and throw away, then cut the flesh into cubes.

Peel the lychees if using fresh ones and remove the stones.

Put the fruit in a saucepan, half cover with water and bring to the boil. Cover and leave to cook over a low heat for 20 minutes. When done, there should be about 3 tablespoons of liquid remaining.

Blend to a smooth purée.

Tip: Since this has been my daughter's favourite compote since she was little, I make it often. You can find frozen pineapple and lychees year round and these are much more practical than fresh fruit.

Cherry and apple compote

For 4 months onwards
Preparation time: 20 minutes
Cooking time: 15 minutes
Makes 5 x 100 g (3½ oz) portions

400 g (14 oz) cherries, stoned
3 large apples, peeled, cored and
   cut into pieces

Put the fruit in a saucepan, half cover with water and bring to the boil. Cover and leave to cook for 15 minutes. When done, there should be about 3 dessertspoons of liquid remaining.

Blend to a smooth purée.

Variation: Out of season, you could replace the cherries with black grapes. Wash, cut in half and remove the seeds if there are any. Use sweeter apples to balance the slight acidity of the grapes.

Plum and pear compote

For 4 months onwards
Preparation time: 15 minutes
Cooking time: 15 minutes
Makes 5 x 100 g (3½ oz) portions

350 g (12¼ oz) plums, stoned
3 sweet pears (e.g. Williams),
   peeled, cored and cut into pieces

Put the fruit in a saucepan, one-third cover with water and bring to the boil. Cover and leave to cook for 15 minutes. When done, there should be about 3 dessertspoons of liquid remaining.

Blend to a smooth purée.

Tip: There are many different types of plum, some more sour than others. Use well-ripened sweet plums as the skin will add a little note of acidity.

Oat cookies

For 12 months onwards
Preparation time: 10 minutes
Cooking time: 10–15 minutes
Makes 16–20 cookies

300 g (10½ oz) oats
100 g (3½ oz) butter, melted
150 g (5¼ oz) brown sugar
150 g (5¼ oz) raisins
200 g (7 oz) plain flour

Preheat the oven to 180°C (fan oven 160°C), Gas Mark 4.

In a bowl, mix the oats and melted butter together.

Add the sugar and raisins, then add the flour little by little. Add 5 dessertspoons of water and mix to a firm paste.

Make small balls of the cookie mixture and place them, spaced 5 cm (2 inches) apart, on a baking tray covered with greaseproof paper. Flatten them gently and cook in the centre of the oven for 10–15 minutes until golden.

Take out of the oven and leave to cool on a cooling rack before serving accompanied by some fresh fruit kebabs.

Variation: If you want a real treat, replace the raisins with chocolate chips.

Thanks

I am truly proud of this book of recipes, which was, until now, nothing more than a workbook, written by hand, worn out and stained. If, today, that workbook has become this book, it is thanks to the help of many people: testers, supporters, sources of inspiration, correcters and all those who put up with me.

A big thank you to Marabout, to Emmanuel and Amaryllis, who gave me the opportunity to write this book, who gave me confidence, and thanks to whom this book is beautiful, personal and unique. Thanks also to Fred and Sonia Lucano for the wonderful photographs, and to the baby models who were so ready to play. And a huge thank you to Cédrine Meier, who, thanks to her formidable talent for writing, helped me make the text readable, relevant and funny.

I also want to pay tribute to my husband David, who, through his support, tolerance and involvement with the family, enabled me to start the mad adventure that is 'baby meals' and to work day and night on this book.

Finally, the biggest of thanks to my children Maya and Milo. You are my reason for living and my inspiration. All this is thanks to you. I love you like crazy!

Jenny

Thanks to White and Brown household goods.

Marabout would like to thank the parents of the children who were so well behaved at the photoshoot.

All the babies were dressed by Lili & the Funky Boys, thank you Esther!

Index

Conversion tables

The tables below are only approximate and are meant to be used as a guide only.

Approximate American/ European conversions

	USA	Metric	Imperial
brown sugar	1 cup	170 g	6 oz
butter	1 stick	115 g	4 oz
butter/ margarine/ lard	1 cup	225 g	8 oz
caster and granulated sugar	2 level tablespoons	30 g	1 oz
caster and granulated sugar	1 cup	225 g	8 oz
currants	1 cup	140 g	5 oz
flour	1 cup	140 g	5 oz
golden syrup	1 cup	350 g	12 oz
ground almonds	1 cup	115 g	4 oz
sultanas/ raisins	1 cup	200 g	7 oz

Approximate American/ European conversions

American	European
1 teaspoon	1 teaspoon/ 5 ml
½ fl oz	1 tablespoon/ ½ fl oz/ 15 ml
¼ cup	4 tablespoons/ 2 fl oz/ 50 ml
½ cup plus 2 tablespoons	¼ pint/ 5 fl oz/ 150 ml
1¼ cups	½ pint/ 10 fl oz/ 300 ml
1 pint/ 16 fl oz	1 pint/ 20 fl oz/ 600 ml
2½ pints (5 cups)	1.2 litres/ 2 pints
10 pints	4.5 litres/ 8 pints

Liquid measures

Imperial	ml	fl oz
1 teaspoon	5	
2 tablespoons	30	
4 tablespoons	60	
¼ pint/ 1 gill	150	5
⅓ pint	200	7
½ pint	300	10
¾ pint	425	15
1 pint	600	20
1¾ pints	1000 (1 litre)	35

Oven temperatures

American	Celsius	Fahrenheit	Gas Mark
Cool	130	250	½
Very slow	140	275	1
Slow	150	300	2
Moderate	160	320	3
Moderate	180	350	4
Moderately hot	190	375	5
Fairly hot	200	400	6
Hot	220	425	7
Very hot	230	450	8
Extremely hot	240	475	9

Other useful measurements

Measurement	Metric	Imperial
1 American cup	225 ml	8 fl oz
1 egg, size 3	50 ml	2 fl oz
1 egg white	30 ml	1 fl oz
1 rounded tablespoon flour	30 g	1 oz
1 rounded tablespoon cornflour	30 g	1 oz
1 rounded tablespoon caster sugar	30 g	1 oz
2 level teaspoons gelatine	10 g	¼ oz

Vera,
16 months,
gourmet

Mona,
6 months,
foodie baby